Cakes, Bakes, Puddings and Prayers

by SUSAN OVER

Foreword by WENDY CRAIG

Published by
The Leprosy Mission International
80 Windmill Road, Brentford
Middlesex TW8 0QH, United Kingdom

Edited and distributed by TLM Trading Limited (address on page 72)

First published 2006, reprinted 2006, second reprint 2007
© Susan Over

Editorial and Design by Creative Plus Publishing Ltd.
2nd Floor, 151 High Street, Billericay, Essex, CM12 9AB
www.creative-plus.co.uk

Printed and bound in China
Phoenix Offset
A catalogue record for this book is available from the British Library.
ISBN 0 902731 61 0

Foreword

Puddings and Prayers – what a lovely idea for a book! My mother taught me to cook and bake when I was quite young. We'd roll out pastry shapes and they'd be quite grey by the time I'd finished – you know what children are like! I used to love making strawberry jam tarts to 'poison' Dad with when he came home from work – it was such fun! And Dad was kind enough not to mention the grey pastry.

Cooking is often very therapeutic and these recipes combine so well with the thoughts and prayers. When I'm in a state I've been known to stop and make marmalade – it's very calming and comforting. Maybe next time I'll try In-a-Flap-Jacks!

Ria, my character in *Butterflies*, was a disaster in the kitchen, but I reckon that even she might manage some of the recipes in this book! The Raspberry Butterflies on page 48 would look super on an Easter tea table and, of course, butterflies remind us of the New Life that Jesus offers to all.

It is some years since I first became involved with The Leprosy Mission and I'm proud to be associated with such a worthwhile cause. It's tremendous to think that the profits from this book will go towards supporting TLM hospitals and workshops abroad. I wish *Cakes, Bakes, Puddings and Prayers* every success.

Happy Baking!

Wendy Craig

Dedication

For Katherine Elizabeth, my daughter, my joy
For Mum, who taught me how to entertain and
For Ern, who lives with my creativity...

Acknowledgements

Photography by Tim Sandall, assisted by Christine Sandall.
All the recipes were tried, tested and baked for photography by
Wendy Dyer, Honor Harris, Susan Over and Judith Merrell.
Thanks also to Katherine Turner.

Personal Thoughts

Honor: I enjoyed baking for the photos in this book. Don't worry if you do not have the exact ingredients for a recipe, find something similar, be relaxed about your cooking and enjoy Sue's meditations.

Tim: I didn't just take the photos, I had to try all the recipes too! *The Eternal Syllabub* was probably my favourite, but I might have to try them all again before I could be sure...

Wendy: I'm delighted with the recipe for *Welcome Rock Cakes*, they really do melt in the mouth. I'll be using this recipe again and again!

Katherine: We are always amused when people try to guess what is in *Chocolate Dream Layer* – my favourite of all Mum's puddings.

Judith: The *Rest and Be Thankful Chocolate Cake* is quite delicious, both my children have requested it for their birthday cake this year!

Christine: It's very hard to choose a favourite cake or dessert, I enjoyed so many of them. The *Sunshine Drizzle Cake* is definitely delicious.

Susan: I'm so pleased that the testers have enjoyed these recipes.
A special 'thank you' to Judith for all her suggestions and encouragement.

Contents

A Different Grumble — 6
Angel Fruit Tartlets — 8
Apostle Cake — 10
Autumn Upside-down Pudding — 12
Blushing Apple Tart — 14
Buried Treasure — 16
Chocolate Dream Layer — 18
Chocolate Silk — 20
Coventry God Cakes — 22
Crafty Pudding — 24
Ern's Coconut Treats — 26
Eternal Syllabub — 28
Flibbertigibbets — 30
Give-and-Take Biscuit Bake — 32
Healthy Apricot Slices — 34
In-a-Flap-Jacks — 36
Lemon Delight Pudding — 38

Make a Date Loaf — 40
Merry Muffins — 42
Mini Melting Moments — 44
Mixed Berry Mess — 46
Raspberry Butterflies — 48
Rest and Be Thankful Chocolate Cake — 50
Scones of Splendour — 52
Speedy Turnovers — 54
Spiced Easter Biscuits — 56
Strawberry Shortbread Hearts — 58
Sunday Sundaes — 60
Sunshine Drizzle Cake — 62
Tea and Sympathy Cake — 64
The Best Ever No-bake Chocolate Slice! — 66
Tumble-down Cake — 68
Welcome Rock Cakes — 70

A Different Grumble

Fruit crumble is a good standby pudding, especially in winter, but it can be awfully boring, thus earning it the nickname 'Apple Grumble' from one little boy visitor... Here's a variation – with some other ideas to try – so we can enjoy a different grumble occasionally!

Wholemeal flour is the healthiest option for the crumble, but if you prefer a lighter topping use 110g (4oz) plain flour.

Alternative fruit bases include: 3 large peeled and sliced cooking apples mixed with 250g (9oz) strawberries; or 410g tin each of pears, drained, and prunes in juice. A more traditional base is rhubarb with a touch of finely grated stem ginger (add ½ teaspoon ground ginger to the crumble mix, too).

Ingredients

For fruit base:
4 or 5 fresh peaches, sliced
200g (7oz) fresh raspberries

For crumble topping:
75g (3oz) butter or margarine
110g (4oz) wholemeal flour
50g (2oz) porridge oats
25-50g (1-2oz) soft brown sugar
A few flaked almonds

Method

1 Preheat oven to gas mark 4/180°C/350°F.
2 Arrange sliced peaches and raspberries in base of medium ovenproof dish.
3 Rub butter into flour in large bowl and when it resembles breadcrumbs, add sugar and oats and mix lightly.
4 Spread crumble mix evenly over the fruit.
5 Sprinkle a few flaked almonds on the top.
6 Bake for 30-40 minutes until browned, and serve hot with custard or single cream.
Serves 4.

> Therefore, encourage one another and build each other up, just as in fact you are doing.
>
> 1 Thessalonians 5:11 (NIV)

Some time ago the only thing I gave up for Lent was criticism. By the end of Ash Wednesday I had caught myself criticising three different people to family and friends. Ouch! Grumbling and mumbling about people and situations is an ingrained habit that many of us find hard to break.

A few years ago I took part in a study course which aimed to build positive relationships in the church. One very useful exercise was 'Avoid harsh criticism once a day'. This was not only achievable but also made us more on our guard for the rest of each day. After all, it was a bit hypocritical to resist pulling last night's sermon apart with my husband, but then do that very thing on the phone to my friend!

Anyone who is in the limelight is likely to come under more scrutiny than the average pew-filler, but do we really expect our leaders to be perfect this side of heaven? They are human like the rest of us with stresses and strains, doubts and fears.

Next time we are about to moan about someone else, why not think about the little rhyme below and see if we can find something positive to say instead?

It can start with just a mumble,
which then becomes a grumble,
causing folks to stumble,
spoiling lives.

Let's remember to be humble,
ignore that petty rumble
and build instead of crumble!
Blessing lives.

Lord, help us to look for the positive instead of dwelling on the negative. And show us new ways to bring your light and vision into situations which now seem dark and dreary. Amen

Angel Fruit Tartlets

These dainty mini tarts are ideal for a buffet or afternoon tea party. The pastry cases can be made up to a couple of days in advance and stored carefully in a tin – or you could buy ready-made pastry. Choose a variety of colourful fruits to make a mouth-watering display.

Assemble as near to serving as possible, as the filling starts to soften the pastry if left too long.

Ingredients

Pastry cases:
175g (6oz) plain flour
75g (3oz) butter
50g (2oz) caster sugar
1 egg yolk

Fillings:
175g (6oz) mascarpone cheese
1 tablespoon caster sugar
1 level teaspoon finely grated orange zest
Various prepared fruits e.g. halved
   seedless grapes; tinned mandarin
   segments; sliced fresh
   strawberries or raspberries;
   tinned or fresh pineapple pieces
Apricot jam, sieved if necessary,
   for glaze.

Method

1 Preheat oven to gas mark 5/190°C/375°F. Lightly grease a shallow 12-hole bun tin.
2 Rub butter into flour until mixture resembles breadcrumbs; stir in sugar.
3 Add egg yolk and enough water to bind into soft dough. Wrap and chill for at least 30 minutes.
4 Roll pastry quite thinly and cut 12 pastry circles to fill the tin. Prick bases with a fork and line each case with foil to prevent rising.
5 Bake for 10 minutes. Remove foil and bake for a further 5-10 minutes until golden.
6 Leave tartlets in tin to cool for a few minutes, then remove carefully and cool on wire rack.
7 Beat cheese with sugar and orange zest until smooth, then divide between cases and arrange fruit on top, either using one variety to one case, or a combination in each.
8 Warm a heaped tablespoon of apricot jam with 1-2 tablespoons of water. Brush over fruit (optional).
9 Chill for a few minutes before serving to allow jam to set.
Makes 12 tartlets.

Are not all angels ministering spirits sent to serve those who will inherit salvation?

Hebrews 1:14 (NIV)

One evening, I was driving to collect my daughter from Girls Brigade when I saw a middle-aged couple, very dignified, but painfully thin and poorly dressed, rummaging in the bin outside a fish and chip shop. They tugged at my heart and on the way home seeing them walking steadily back along the country road, I jumped out of the car and asked if they could use some money. I gave them more than I could easily afford at that time but the look of gratitude in the woman's eyes has stayed with me to this day.

There was something other-worldly about that couple and I have often wondered if they were angels sent to teach me another lesson about dependency on God since we did not miss that amount at all. In fact, we received it back twofold when a friend sent an unexpected gift.

An Internet site offers a quick-fix Personal Life Plan to teach you how to get in touch with your angel – for a large fee, of course! Another wants to 'pass on their joy and love of Angels' by selling us an expensive garden ornament. But this is just a tacky commercial enterprise and nothing to do with God's very real angels.

A study of angels in the Bible proves fascinating. They are, in fact, created beings, quite distinct from humans, who are used by God as messengers. For instance, in the Old Testament angels tell Abraham that Sarah will have a baby in her old age (Genesis 18:10). And in the New Testament an angel foretells Jesus' birth to Mary and Joseph separately (Luke 1:26-33 and Matthew 1:20). Later after Jesus' death an angel tells the women at the tomb that Jesus has risen (Mark 16:6-7).

So let's be clear that angels are real – not airy-fairy creatures drifting around in limbo but co-existing with us to do the Father's will here on earth. And, as the writer to the Hebrews says, 'Do not forget to entertain strangers, for by so doing some people have entertained angels without knowing it'. Hebrews 13:2.

Lord, it is exciting to realise afresh that we are surrounded by your angels.
Help us to keep our ears and eyes open to receive the messages you send
and show us how to work with the angels to build your kingdom here on earth. Amen

Apostle Cake

This is a new version of the traditional Simnel Cake and would make an interesting conversation piece for Easter Sunday tea. The eleven balls of marzipan represent the remaining disciples after Judas has betrayed Jesus and left his companions.

 Keep the egg shells so you can use any remaining whites to fix the marzipan balls in place.

 Tie a bright yellow ribbon around the circumference to make an attractive cake for your Easter tea table.

Ingredients
175g (6oz) butter or margarine
175g (6oz) golden caster sugar
3 medium eggs
110g (4oz) plain wholemeal flour
110g (4oz) self-raising white flour
110g (4oz) Brazil nuts, chopped
175g (6oz) ready-to-eat dried apricots, chopped
50g (2oz) mixed candied peel
2 tablespoons apricot jam
454g (1lb) pack of marzipan
1–2 tablespoons milk

Method
1 Preheat oven to gas mark 4/180°C/350°F. Grease and line a deep 20cm (8in) cake tin.
2 Cream butter or margarine and sugar together until light and fluffy. Gradually beat in eggs with a little sifted flour to prevent curdling.
3 Sift flours together and fold into mixture with any bran left in sieve from wholemeal flour, nuts, apricots and candied peel. Add milk.
4 Turn half the cake mixture into the tin, roll out about one third of the marzipan and place on top, then add the rest of the mixture. Bake for 1-1¼ hours or until cake springs back when pressed. Leave in tin for a few minutes, then turn out and cool on wire rack.
5 Sieve and warm apricot jam; spread over top of cake.
6 Roll out the remaining marzipan. Place the cake tin over the top and cut round it to produce a neat circle to fit top of cake.
7 Divide the trimmings into eleven equal pieces and roll into balls to represent the disciples. Apply a whole beaten egg wash over the cake, then fix the balls in place and egg wash these.
8 Toast under grill or with a kitchen blow torch.
Makes 10-12 slices.

On the evening of that first day of the week, when the disciples were together,
… Jesus came and stood among them and said, 'Peace be with you!'

John 20:19 (NIV)

Simnel Cake has its roots in medieval England. Some say it is from the Latin for a fine flour called 'simla'. A more colourful version is that a brother and sister, Simon and Nell, were making a cake to take home to their mother. They couldn't agree on the method – whether to boil it or bake it – so they compromised and the result was a stodgy confection! My version is lighter, I promise.

How would we react today to something like Jesus' appearance in the Upper Room after his amazing resurrection, I wonder? The news would be flashed round the world in moments and everyone would have an opinion. There would be sceptics who would dismiss the resurrection as a conjuring trick or rationalise it by saying Jesus was only in a coma and revived in the coolness of the tomb. Perhaps the disciples would be offered treatment for post-traumatic stress – if they were believed.

At school I was taught by a liberal Christian who explained away all the miracles in the Bible. At the time it made sense, but as I have grown into my faith, the only thing that makes real sense now is the absolute otherness of Jesus. Far from believing that science takes us further away from a Creator God, I see God as the ultimate scientist, whose mind we will understand more fully when we reach heaven.

So what about Judas, the missing apostle? Was he pre-destined to betray Jesus to the Roman authorities, or did he simply let his greed get the better of him? Either way he couldn't live with what he had done.

And doubting Thomas who had to have proof of Jesus' return from the dead? Well, he is still there among the eleven true apostles – which gives me hope. We may not feel 100% sure of our faith at times. But God never stops believing in us and is always there when we choose to turn back to him.

Praise you, Jesus, that you died and came back from the dead so I could have eternal life.
Lord, I look forward to your coming again when we will see you in all your glory. Amen

Autumn Upside-down Pudding

A hearty, warming pudding – good to serve on Harvest Sunday with custard
or clotted cream. Any leftovers can be sliced and eaten as cake.

 Decorate with blackberry leaves if available.

Ingredients

275g (10oz) fresh or defrosted blackberries,
  drained of any excess moisture
50g (2oz) medium oatmeal
25g (1oz) caster sugar
110g (4oz) margarine or butter
225g (8oz) self-raising flour
110g (4oz) soft brown sugar
200ml (7fl oz) milk
1 large egg

Method

1 Preheat oven to gas mark 4/180°C/350°F. Lightly grease
  a medium-sized glass casserole dish or cake tin.
2 Place blackberries in base of dish or tin.
3 Mix oatmeal and caster sugar together and sprinkle
  over blackberries.
4 Rub margarine or butter into flour and brown sugar until
  mixture resembles fine breadcrumbs.
5 Beat milk and egg together and blend into dry mixture until
  smooth, then spoon this mixture over the fruit and smooth
  the surface.
6 Bake for 1 hour until well risen and golden.
7 Allow to stand for a couple of minutes, then turn onto
  a plate and serve warm.

Serves 6.

(The Lord is)... like an eagle that stirs up its nest and hovers over its young,
that spreads its wings to catch them and carries them on its pinions.

Deuteronomy 32:11 (NIV)

I once knew an elderly woman who could not come to terms with widowhood when her husband died after a long illness. Childless, they had been everything to each other and she had depended utterly on him for all kinds of practical as well as emotional support.

Now her life was turned upside-down and she believed it could never be righted again until she joined her husband. Sadly, although she attended church, she felt no assurance of salvation and could not accept the help of Christians and, through them, of the Lord.

At some point most families will experience something that turns life upside-down, whether it is sudden death, unexpected redundancy, serious illness or some other event that is unique to their particular family. My extended family suffered a number of ordeals over a short space of time which left some of us feeling terribly bruised and battered. Only our strong faith brought us through that trauma.

In his book *The Divine Eagle* (CWR 1988) Selwyn Hughes uses the imagery of the caring mother eagle who tips her young out of their comfortable nest when it is time for them to learn to fly; just as they are about to hit the ground squawking with fright, she swoops down and carries them back to safety on her broad wings.

Whilst tragedy is part of the human condition, the Lord has a wonderful way of using every experience to draw us closer to him and make us more effective Christians. When we have undergone deep personal loss or other distress, we can more readily empathise with others even though our experience may not be exactly the same as theirs. As Selwyn puts it 'the deprivations we experience motivate us towards greater usefulness'.

Just as the pudding has to be turned upside-down to show its best side, so the Lord sometimes allows our lives to be turned over to reveal his glory as he walks with us through our valleys and brings us back to the mountain top.

Lord, make us more aware that you walk with us through the valleys as well as rejoice with us on the mountain tops. Show us how to trust you more when life seems to be turned upside-down and keep us praising, Lord. Amen

Blushing Apple Tart

This is a welcome variation on an old favourite and makes an attractive warm or cold dessert. You may prefer to make your own pastry.

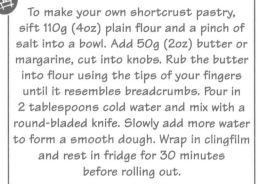

To make your own shortcrust pastry, sift 110g (4oz) plain flour and a pinch of salt into a bowl. Add 50g (2oz) butter or margarine, cut into knobs. Rub the butter into flour using the tips of your fingers until it resembles breadcrumbs. Pour in 2 tablespoons cold water and mix with a round-bladed knife. Slowly add more water to form a smooth dough. Wrap in clingfilm and rest in fridge for 30 minutes before rolling out.

Ingredients
110g (4oz) butter
110g (4oz) light soft brown sugar
2 tablespoons clear honey or golden syrup
4 medium-sized red-skinned eating apples, such as Royal Gala, Empire or Cox's
250g (9oz) ready-made shortcrust pastry

Method
1 Preheat oven gas mark 6/200°C/400°F.
2 Melt butter, sugar and honey or golden syrup in large pan over a moderate heat, stirring until dissolved. Remove from heat.
3 Core and quarter apples leaving peel on, then turn them in the caramel sauce. Replace on heat and simmer gently for 2 minutes.
4 Roll out pastry on a lightly floured board and cut out a circle using a deep flan tin, 23cm (9in) circumference, as your guide.
5 Arrange apples, skin side down, in flan tin and pour over half the caramel sauce.
6 Place pastry circle over apples and press down edges.
7 Bake for 20–25 minutes until pastry is golden.
8 Remove from oven and allow to stand for 5 minutes. Place large serving plate over tin and invert carefully so that apples are uppermost.
9 Serve with remaining warmed caramel sauce and cream, ice-cream or Greek yogurt.
Serves 6.

> ...they have no shame at all; they do not even know how to blush.
>
> Jeremiah 6:15 (NIV)

What makes you blush?

Last Christmas night, ten of us aged from seven to 83 were watching a TV programme which some of us found hilarious while others shrank down in our seats deeply embarrassed. Conscious of the innocence of the youngest and the sensibilities of the eldest, but not wanting to offend the middle group, I went to do the washing up...

We live in an age of familiarity and immodesty. Little girls wearing provocative clothes like their pop idols... Soap mums encouraging their teenagers to move in with their partners... Vile language and graffiti on the streets... What used to be considered immoral is now the norm. It is incredibly hard to stand up and be counted as a Christian in an age where morality and decency are so de-valued.

The popular wristband slogan 'WWJD?' – What would Jesus do? – has been a great encouragement to lots of young (and older) people in our church reminding us of principles that are not only God's law but also basically healthy.

My own past is too chequered for me to judge anyone else but I know how easy it is to justify one's actions to oneself. How I must have grieved the Lord and others who loved me. Thank goodness he forgives us when we are truly sorry and turn back to him.

I used to struggle with the line in The Lord's Prayer about temptation; as if the Lord would deliberately lead us to a place where we would find it difficult to resist wrongdoing. Then an old and wise Christian explained that he thought there should be an extra comma so that it reads, 'And lead us, not into temptation, but deliver us from evil...' The emphasis then is less on struggling and striving, but on following the Lord's leading along positive paths to real fulfilment and joy.

Never be afraid to blush – it shows you are still sensitive! And as Mark Twain says, 'Man is the only animal that blushes. Or needs to.'

Lord, you are an awesome God and we should fall on our knees in wonder and praise at your greatness. Thank you for becoming like one of us so that you feel our human weakness and understand our struggles. Help us to be strong in a world that has strayed so far from you and keep us sensitive to the prompting of your Spirit. Amen

Buried Treasure

This is an excellent quick – and – easy pudding for summer evenings. The sharpness of the yogurt contrasts with the sweetness of the topping and the 'treasure'.

For a more sophisticated version, soak 50g (2oz) raisins in rum for 2 hours and add to bananas, reducing the amount of fudge or sugar.

Ingredients
2 or 3 large bananas
2-3 squares of plain fudge
  or 50g (2oz) soft brown sugar
284ml carton double cream
275g (10oz) Greek yogurt
50-75g (2-3oz) icing sugar

Method
1 Slice bananas and place in a deep heatproof serving dish, approximately 21cm x 16cm (8in x 6in). Either chop fudge into small dice and sprinkle over bananas, or sprinkle with soft brown sugar.

2 Whip cream and yogurt together until thick and spread over fruit, keeping surface as level as possible. Chill for at least 1 hour.

3 Dust with half the icing sugar and place under preheated grill for 3-4 minutes until sugar caramelises (watch carefully), or use a kitchen blowtorch. Repeat with remaining icing sugar.

4 Chill for a few minutes until topping is crisp, and serve within an hour to prevent caramel from softening.
Serves 6.

The kingdom of heaven is like treasure hidden in a field. When a man found it, he hid it again, and then in his joy went and sold all he had and bought that field.

Matthew 13:44 (NIV)

What do you treasure? Have you ever done the exercise where you imagine what you would grab first if your house was on fire (not counting other humans)? Some have said their pets, others photos or precious mementoes. I thought our friend, Dave, who said his paperwork so that he could contact the insurance company quickly, had great presence of mind! Personally, I would be devastated if my computer went up in flames...

The Bible uses the image of treasure quite often in both the Old and New Testaments. For example the writer of Proverbs compares wisdom to a treasure like silver and encourages us to search for it (Proverbs 2:4 and 5). Wisdom is valuable and something we cannot lose through fire or flood. Perhaps we need to hold on less tightly to material objects or even people and relationships if they are in danger of becoming our idols.

Jesus tells us (Matthew 6:19-21) not to set too much store by earthly treasure or material possessions, but to build up our treasure in heaven by trying to be the people he meant us to be as we travel towards eternity.

When I first met my second husband I was delighted – and a little envious – that he often addressed his young grand-daughters as 'Treasure' or 'Treas'. No one had ever called me that! Now occasionally I get called this too and it is a reminder that to God each one of us is His Treasure – someone to be valued, cared for and delighted in.

Help us, Lord, to appreciate that we are your treasure and to live in the light of that amazing truth. Teach us to store up the best kind of treasure in Heaven by our words and deeds. And thank you, Lord, that our greatest treasure is the gift of your son, Jesus. Amen

17

Chocolate Dream Layer

Whenever there is a Bring and Share meal at church or amongst family and friends I am asked to make this pudding. First-time tasters are usually baffled by the main ingredient – bread. Have a go and watch it become a favourite in your circle, too.

Use half the ingredients for a family-sized dessert. It can be made up to a day in advance.

Ingredients

5-6 slices fresh wholemeal or granary bread, crumbed in the liquidiser
225g (8oz) drinking chocolate
2 teaspoons coffee powder (if using granules, grind them down on a saucer with the back of a spoon)
50g (2oz) demerara sugar (or less if preferred)
568ml (1 pint/20fl oz) double or whipping cream
1–2 tablespoons milk
Crushed chocolate flake to decorate

Method

1 Mix together breadcrumbs, drinking chocolate, coffee powder and sugar in a bowl until the breadcrumbs are well coated.
2 Whisk cream and milk together in another bowl until it just holds soft peaks (don't make it too stiff).
3 Starting with the chocolate mixture, layer into a glass serving dish, finishing with the cream. Decorate with the crushed flake.
4 Chill until ready to serve.
Serves 8.

I am a dreamer. Probably because of an over-fertile imagination there are few nights that go by when I do not dream in amazing technicolour. Depending on my state of mind and the events of the day I can wake refreshed, puzzled or disturbed by these dreams.

At times I have kept a Dream Diary and tried to trace why a person I have not consciously thought of for decades has suddenly appeared doing something strange in my dream. Often there is no apparent reason and then I just say a quick prayer for that person in case God has planted him or her there for just that reason.

God's dramatic promise to Jacob in his dream of a stairway up to heaven (Genesis 28:12) and the warning to Joseph to take the baby Jesus beyond the reach of murderous Herod (Matthew 2:19) are just two examples of the way God uses dreams to speak directly to his people. Using our conscious minds to dream of ways we can work with our Father for a better world can be a powerful tool in outreach. The world needs dreamers – people who truly listen to the inward promptings of the Spirit during the day and in the night.

When I named this pudding I included Dream in the title because when people taste it, they often go 'mmmm' and get that faraway look in their eyes! Dreams and daydreams are great but they have to be put into practice. Just as we have to continue to eat the pudding to appreciate its taste, so we must continue to 'taste and see that the Lord is good' and share that goodness with those around us.

Make me a dreamer for your kingdom, Lord; help me to see the world through your eyes and do all
I can to bring it in line with your will. Speak to me, Lord, through your creation and my imagination. Amen

Chocolate Silk

This smooth silky dream of a dessert would be ideal for an intimate meal for two, but could also be increased for a dinner party.

Chocolate shapes give a professional look and are easy to make. Place a couple of squares of chocolate in one corner of a plastic food bag and melt in microwave for a few seconds. Snip one corner off the bag and drizzle chocolate onto baking parchment to make knot or fan shapes. Set in fridge.

Ingredients
60ml (2fl oz) milk
1 heaped teaspoon instant coffee granules
50g (2oz) plain chocolate
50g (2oz) milk chocolate
1 egg
1 scant tablespoon brandy or whisky (optional)
Whipped cream and grated chocolate to decorate

Method
1 Chop chocolate into small pieces.
2 Heat milk and coffee together in a small pan or microwave until just below boiling point.
3 Pour milk mixture into blender and add chocolate.
4 Blend for about half a minute.
5 Separate egg and add yolk and spirit to mixture. Blend again until smooth.
6 In a large bowl, whisk egg white until stiff, then fold in the chocolate mixture until well blended.
7 Pour into individual glass dishes and chill for at least three hours.
8 Decorate with whipped cream and flake before serving.
Serves 2.

NB This recipe includes raw egg and therefore should not be given to pregnant women or the very elderly.

> **A good woman is hard to find, and worth far more than diamonds…
> She makes her own clothing, and dresses in colourful linens and silks.**
> Proverbs 31:10, 22 (The Message)

A couple of years ago I discovered silk and it led to a surprising career change. I now run a small business painting silk scarves, cushions, ties and cards and speaking to all sorts of groups about the history of silk and how it is made.

Silk has always been a luxury fabric and highly prized. The Chinese kept the manufacture of it a closely guarded secret for 3,000 years and Julius Caesar liked it so much that he would only let his family and senate wear it.

Silk is warm, strong and flexible and has been used in such unusual items as bicycle tyres. I was assured by one customer that wearing a silk scarf would cure a sore throat in a couple of days and by another that it was used to strengthen the Great Wall of China, though I'm not too sure about that!

The best thing about silk for me is its feel-good factor. Literally, it feels soft and caressing to the touch and is a joy to give to someone special.

Reading the whole *Hymn to a Good Wife* in Proverbs 31 we get a picture of a woman who is not just hard-working and making the most of her natural talents but is also trustworthy, generous and, above all, God-fearing. Though she spends most of her time working for her family, she's well-organised and manages to be elegant. And she 'faces tomorrow with a smile'. A model for all of us!

So, when we give something special to someone we care about – whether it is a silk scarf or a Chocolate Silk pudding – let's aspire to come up to the standards of that lovely woman in Proverbs and do it with her grace and generosity!

Lord, help me to be a better wife, mother, friend. Help me to share the best things of life with others so that your love is reflected through me to them. Amen

Coventry God Cakes

Mentioned by Chaucer, the triangular shape of these God Cakes is a variation on a theme like the dried fruit pastries such as Eccles, Chorley or Banbury Cakes that crop up in different areas of Britain.

 These 'cakes' also work well with shortcrust pastry.

 If you have time, prepare the fruit mixture in advance and allow to cool and set, this makes it easier to divide between the pastry shapes.

Ingredients

500g (1lb 2oz) ready-made puff pastry
50g (2oz) butter
275g (10oz) mixed dried fruit
1 heaped teaspoon mixed spice
½ teaspoon ground cinnamon
50g (2oz) demerara sugar
1 tablespoon brandy
Egg white and caster sugar for glaze

Method

1 Preheat oven to gas mark 7/220°C/425°F.
2 Roll pastry to approximate thickness of a 2p piece. Cut into 12 squares.
3 Melt butter and add fruit, spices, sugar and brandy, mix well.
4 Place a dessertspoonful of mixture on each pastry shape and fold to make triangles, damping edges with water to seal.
5 Place on lightly greased baking tray, flattening slightly, and make short cut in top of each to allow steam to escape.
6 Brush with lightly beaten egg white and sprinkle with sugar.
7 Bake for about 10 minutes until golden.
8 Cool on tray for a few minutes then finish on wire rack.
Makes 12.

> As soon as Jesus was baptised, he went up out of the water. At that moment heaven was opened, and he saw the Spirit of God descending like a dove and lighting on him. And a voice from heaven said, 'This is my Son, whom I love; with him I am well pleased.'
>
> Matthew 3.16-17 (NIV)

Coventry God Cakes were made in the shape of triangles in honour of the Trinity and were given by godparents to children on New Year's Day.

Did you know that the Trinity as such does not occur in the Bible? There is no verse in which the three-in-one God is mentioned and yet in Matthew 28:18 Jesus tells his followers to 'go and make disciples of all nations, baptising them in the name of the Father and of the Son and of the Holy Spirit'.

It is an idea that is sometimes difficult to get our heads round. How could Father God, the Creator, come to earth and call himself his own Son? But Jesus makes it clear that he is in the Father and the Father is in him (John 14:11). And what about the Holy Spirit? Before his death and resurrection, Jesus promises his disciples that his Father will send the Counsellor, the Holy Spirit in his place. It's like nothing else we know.

I don't believe we are intended to understand all the mystery of God until we get to heaven. There are dimensions that we cannot fully appreciate with our finite minds. And that is what faith is all about – considering all the evidence and then trusting God for all the gaps in our understanding.

Going back to the cakes... Isn't it a good thing when we give each other reminders of our faith? My Mum collects those little cards with Scripture verses and inspirational poems on them and has often encouraged me with one at just the right time.

A book of Bible stories or prayers for children, given at a christening or dedication, may not be read for a few years but could be a step on the way to that child finding faith for himself.

Lord, we may never fully understand the mystery of you this side of eternity but thank you for those who teach and encourage us in your ways. May we always be willing to point others to you and encourage them to learn more and more about you. Amen

Crafty Mandarin Pudding

When I was a child, an uncle arrived for dinner unexpectedly. Having no pudding, Mum crumbled the last slices of a Victoria Sponge into a bowl and smothered it with custard. Uncle Jim dubbed it Crafty Pudding and ever since any hastily made standby has gone by that name.

Ingredients

50g (2oz) butter or margarine
2 eggs
150ml (¼ pint) milk
50g (2oz) sugar
1 teaspoon vanilla essence
225g (8oz) tin mandarin segments
4 slices 'day old' thick granary bread, or use white bread if you prefer
4-6 squares of plain chocolate for decoration

Method

1 Melt butter or margarine in a medium-sized casserole dish in the microwave for about 30-40 seconds.
2 Add eggs and beat well.
3 Stir in the milk, sugar, vanilla essence and drained mandarins. Mix well.
4 Remove the crusts from the bread, cut into cubes and stir into the mixture. Leave to stand for about 5 minutes.
5 Microwave on FULL power for 5-6 minutes or until set.
6 Melt the chocolate in the microwave on LOW power for 1 minute, then drizzle or zigzag it over the top.
7 Allow to cool for a couple of minutes before serving with vanilla ice-cream or single cream.

Serves 3–4.

> Do not be anxious about anything, but in everything, by prayer and petition,
> with thanksgiving, present your requests to God.
>
> Philippians 4:6 (NIV)

One of my besetting sins is WORRY. One Sunday morning I was agonising over the fear that my craft business would take a drastic slump after Christmas, when I sensed the Lord conducting this conversation with me:

'Have you eaten well over the last 24 hours?'
'Yes Lord. I've had three good meals and treats in between.'
'Have you clothes to wear today?'
'Yes Lord. So many I don't know which to put on.'
'Have you anything to put on the Offering Plate?'
'Yes Lord, it's already in its envelope.'
'Don't you have some holiday coming up?'
'Er, yes Lord. It's booked and paid for.'
'And, my foolish, much-loved child, have I ever let you down before?'
'No, Lord, never.'
'Then stop worrying and live today to the best of your ability.'

Over the years, like St Paul, I have known plenty and I have known want. But, as he reminded me, God has always provided, sometimes in the most unexpected ways. When my daughter was about seven, I was struggling with how I could give her a birthday party as a single parent on a shoestring budget. One morning, a dozen free circus tickets landed on the doormat. My father and a friend ferried two car loads of excited little girls to the circus in the next town and Mum provided fish fingers and chips for all on our return.

Though I asked all the obvious people, no-one ever admitted to sending those tickets and no-one else in our block received any.

Thinking about Crafty Pudding made me realise again that when we have seemingly come to the end of our own resources, we need to be willing both to depend on God and to use the gifts he has given.

P.S. Seen on a church noticeboard: Don't let worry kill you. Let the Church help.

Father, thank you for who you are and thank you for all you have done and will do for me;
forgive me for forgetting your promises so often and worrying about tomorrow unnecessarily.
Help me to live today relaxing in your love and resting in your care. Amen

Ern's Coconut Treats

Coconut macaroons, coconut tartlets, coconut ice-cream
– my husband loves them all. This is a rather rich recipe, which
I only make occasionally – just for a treat! The finished
cakes are sticky, chewy and very yummy.

Washing and drying the fruit helps to
prevent it from sticking together and
sinking to the bottom of the mixture
during baking.

Ingredients

110g (4oz) margarine
175g (6oz) caster sugar
110g (4oz) glacé cherries
110g (4oz) sultanas
175g (6oz) desiccated coconut
50g (2oz) plain flour
2 medium eggs
175g (6oz) plain chocolate

Method

1 Preheat oven gas mark 4/180°C/350°F. Line a Swiss
   roll tin 28cm x 17.5cm (11in x 7in) with greaseproof paper.
2 Cream margarine and sugar until light and fluffy.
3 Wash, dry and chop cherries, and add to mixture with
   sultanas, coconut, flour and eggs. Mix well.
4 Spread mixture in tin and bake in centre of oven for
   30-40 minutes until golden. Turn upside down onto a wire
   cooling rack.
5 When cold, remove the greaseproof paper. Melt the
   chocolate on a LOW setting in the microwave and spread
   over the surface, making a wavy pattern
   with a fork.
6 Cut into 16 pieces with a warm knife once the chocolate
   is set.
   Makes 16 squares.

'Let them give thanks to the LORD for his unfailing love and his wonderful deeds for men,
for he satisfies the thirsty and fills the hungry with good things.'

Psalm 107:8-9 (NIV)

One of my friends used to feel guilty every time she 'treated' herself to anything that wasn't strictly necessary, whether it was something frivolous to wear or a cream cake or chocolate bar. The trouble was she made others feel guilty too if they indulged themselves!

'Naughty but nice' was an effective advertising slogan that we still use today suggesting that anything we really enjoy is sinful. Sometimes we don't realise that when Jesus says the second most important commandment is 'to love our neighbours as ourselves' it presupposes that we value ourselves.

Many of us suffer with such low self-esteem that we don't believe we are worthy of receiving God's love, never mind little treats. But each one of us is so precious to God that he let his only son suffer and die in our place.

Of course we should look after the needs of others, be good stewards of all the Lord entrusts to us, treat our bodies with respect. But so should we enjoy the good things of life in moderation. I'm sure Martha made up a batch of Jesus' favourite sweetmeats when she knew he was coming over. And Mary probably served them up with a secret smile.

As we've grown older, I think both my friend and I have learned to accept the Lord's bounty (no pun intended!) with more grace. We have both realised that we can look after others best when we first recognise our own worth.

Lord, thank you that we have so much to choose from and that we have more than the bare necessities
of life. Please point out different ways that we can make those around us feel special. Amen

Eternal Syllabub

Originally, syllabub was produced when dairymaids directed warm milk straight from the cow onto sherry, or cider, in a pail. The froth was skimmed off, making a delicious and rather alcoholic dish sometimes eaten for breakfast!

This modern recipe makes a thicker and longer-lasting syllabub, which is called 'eternal' because it keeps its shape for several hours and so can be made in advance.

Method

1 Finely grate the zest of the lemon and then squeeze out the juice. Soak the zest in this juice for 2 hours.
2 Mix juice with sugar, brandy and wine or sherry, stirring until the sugar dissolves.
3 Whisk cream lightly until it just begins to hold its shape, then gradually add liquid while continuing to whisk. Do not over-beat.
4 Chill before serving in four individual glass dishes, decorated with a twist of lemon peel and/or a lemon balm leaf or similar.
Serves 4.

Ingredients

1 lemon
75g (3oz) caster sugar
1-2 tablespoons brandy
2 tablespoons sweet dessert wine or sherry
284 ml (10fl oz) double cream
Lemon balm leaves or similar to decorate (optional)

> The eternal God is your refuge, and underneath are the everlasting arms.
>
> Deuteronomy 33:27 (NIV)

When the much-loved father of a friend died during her teens, her simple Christian faith made a deep impact on me. As her eyes shone with tears she quoted a phrase which I often recall:

'In the face of eternity, what does it matter?'

My friend was able to support her mother and younger sister through their time of grief because she knew that her Dad was waiting in heaven for them. That little saying can also help to put everyday problems into perspective.

In the face of eternity... how much does it matter that our brand new car had its back smashed in? Thank you, Lord, that no-one was injured.

In the face of eternity... what does it matter that the washing machine has just flooded? I'm grateful not to have to wash clothes in the river.

In the face of eternity... how much does it matter that a close friend has failed to understand and meet my current need? She has pressing problems of her own.

Little disappointments, small grievances as well as bigger losses and tragedies tend to lose some of their edge when we put them into the broader spectrum of a joyful eternity with our Lord.

Next time you feel life threatening to overwhelm you, try saying that phrase – and see if it makes a difference.

Lord, it's easy to get bogged down in the trials and trivialities of life. Help us to remember that we are looking forward to an eternity with you, where we will be lost in wonder, love and praise. Amen

Flibbertigibbets

These biscuits take their name from a song in *The Sound of Music*!
They are easy to make and children will enjoy helping out, but take care around hot pans.

Ingredients

110g (4oz) margarine
150g (5oz) soft brown sugar
1 tablespoon golden syrup
110g (4oz) self-raising flour
350g (12oz) porridge oats
1 teaspoon bicarbonate of soda
1 medium egg
Milk chocolate, melted, for
   coating (optional)

Method

1 Preheat oven to gas mark 4/180°C/350°F.
2 Melt margarine, sugar and syrup in a medium-sized pan.
3 Add dry ingredients and the egg, then mix well.
4 Form into about 24 walnut-sized balls and space out on two greased baking trays, pressing down with a fork to flatten.
5 Bake for 10–15 minutes until golden.
6 Cool on a wire rack.
7 The biscuits can be half-dipped in melted chocolate, if liked. Lay on baking parchment or greaseproof paper to set.

Makes 24 biscuits.

Perseverance must finish its work so that you may be mature and complete, not lacking anything.

James 1:4 (NIV)

Poor Maria, the would-be nun played by Julie Andrews in *The Sound of Music*. Though they loved her, the other sisters thought of her as 'a flibbertigibbet, a will o' the wisp, a clown'!

Maria Von Trapp, as she would become, was a devout woman trying hard to do God's will, but in the Abbey she was a square peg in a round hole and so she could not settle.

The definition of flibbertigibbet is a 'frivolous, flighty or excessively talkative person'. People can appear to be like that when they are covering up deep insecurities. Do you know anyone like that?

There are the people who church-hop, going from place to place looking for the ideal setting to worship and never finding it. (They can't have taken on board the saying 'If you find the perfect church don't join it, or it won't be perfect anymore'.)

Or those who join in a project enthusiastically at the start but easily become discouraged as time goes on and soon give up altogether.

What about the person who makes promises they never keep?

We recently studied the spiritual gifts again in our Home Group and it was fascinating to see how people saw themselves. Some were sure of God's calling and we all agreed that they were exercising their gifts correctly for the benefit of the whole church. Others said they hadn't yet identified their gifts and we struggled to convince them that being open and willing to do what God asks will help them to feel more sure of their role.

Testing out areas of service until you find your strength is all part of a learning curve. When Maria became governess to the children she was happy – until she fell in love with their father and believed it was wrong. It took the Mother Superior of her convent to convince her that we must climb every mountain until we are sure of our dream.

Lord, as we struggle sometimes to find your will, as we flit about trying to fit into our niche,
help us to listen to your voice through your Word and the prompting of your Spirit.
Then we can be sure of being in the right place in your plan. Amen

Give-and-Take Biscuit Bake

This is a different idea either for fundraising or simply to have a variety of home-made biscuits with minimum work. Three friends, or a parent and two children, could each take a third of the biscuit dough and make a version of the basic recipe. Double the ingredients to use with a bigger group, eg Girls' Brigade or Youth Club.

Ingredients

225g (8oz) butter
110g (4oz) caster sugar
110g (4oz) soft brown sugar
1 standard egg, beaten
½ teaspoon vanilla essence
225g (8oz) self-raising flour

Possible flavourings:

50g (2oz) desiccated coconut
50g (2oz) dried ready-to-eat cranberries
½ teaspoon each ground cinnamon and nutmeg
25g (1oz) chocolate, chopped
25g (1oz) glacé cherries, chopped
50g (2oz) crushed salted peanuts
50g (2oz) ground almonds
1 drop almond essence

Method

1 Cream butter and two sugars until light and fluffy.
2 Gradually beat in the eggs and vanilla essence, then stir in the flour.
3 Divide the mixture into three equal portions and add one of the flavourings to each one, kneading until evenly combined.
4 Shape each flavoured mixture into a roll about 5cm (2in) diameter. Freeze for at least 2 hours to make the mixture firm enough to slice; although it can be kept in the freezer for several weeks.
5 Preheat oven to gas mark 5/190°C/375°F.
6 Cut each frozen roll into 20-24 thin slices and bake on lightly greased baking trays for 10-15 minutes until golden brown.
7 Allow to cool and harden for a couple of minutes, then remove carefully to a wire rack to finish.
8 Store in an airtight tin.

Makes 35-40 biscuits.

Make sure you don't take things for granted and go slack in working
for the common good; share what you have with others.

Hebrews 13:16 (The Message)

Eight of us from three different families blocked the aisle of a supermarket in Cornwall as we argued over which toilet rolls to buy. (The dog wasn't allowed in or doubtless he'd have had an opinion too...)

No, this wasn't another of my weird dreams – this was the start of a long-anticipated first holiday with close friends.

On the whole we had a wonderful week, but it was definitely an exercise in give-and-take. Yet another frustrating moment was trying to find a pub that served meals for hungry men, figure-conscious women and picky children – on foot...

But there were great times too. Like the hilarious picnic on a cliff top in a force nine gale when the food to be shared was in two separate cars... And the game of *Cheat* round the log fire in the evenings when Sid invented his own unusual way of cheating...

We shared the children too, with one adult organising an elaborate treasure hunt and another taking them to see a film while the rest had a break. We found that living together for just that one week provided a great opportunity to get to know each other better – and to learn to be willing to compromise.

Jesus said 'Love one another. As I have loved you, so you must love one another. By this all men will know that you are my disciples, if you love one another' (John 13:34 NIV). He knew that it was easy to love when everything was going well, but somewhat harder when rubbing along in close contact and in unfamiliar circumstances.

A couple of years after the holiday, I moved away from the area and didn't see the friends for several years, but when we met up recently there was still a twinkle in Sid's eye as we reminisced – and yes, I doubt if we'll ever manage to agree about environmentally friendly loo rolls...

Lord, thank you for the joy of human relationships. Help us to celebrate our differences rather than to want our own way all the time. Give us a double dose of 'give-and-take' for today. Amen

Healthy Apricot Slices

Puddings are often 'naughty but nice'. These slices offer a healthier alternative with high fibre and low refined sugar whilst still satisfying that need to finish off a meal with something sweet.

 175g (6oz) dried dates can be simmered in a little water to soften them, and then used as the middle layer instead of the apricots.

 For a richer flavour, though a less healthy option, use butter instead of margarine.

Ingredients
150g (5oz) jumbo or porridge oats
150g (5oz) wholemeal flour
110g (4oz) soft light brown sugar
1 level teaspoon baking powder
175g (6oz) polyunsaturated margarine
175g (6oz) ready-to-eat dried apricots, roughly chopped

Method
1 Preheat oven to gas mark 4/350°F/180°C.
2 Place oats, flour, sugar and baking powder in a bowl and rub in margarine.
3 Put half mixture into a 17cm x 17cm (7in x 7in) tin and press down.
4 Arrange apricots on top, then finish off with remaining mixture, pressing down firmly.
5 Bake for 35 minutes until golden.
6 Cool in tin before cutting into 12 slices.

Makes 12.

If you come with us, we will share with you whatever good things the LORD gives us.

Numbers 10:32 (NIV)

A sentence from a radio bulletin stuck in my mind: 'Half the world has a problem with obesity while the other half starves'.

I was brought up in a family that showed love by force-feeding! Grandad was a whiz with a frying pan. Steak, sausages, bacon, black pudding, eggs, Davy Crocketts – his version of potato croquettes – and this was just for breakfast. Sadly, I developed the habit of trying to solve every problem with food, something I battle with to this day.

The media bombards us with advice on healthy eating and there is no excuse today for not eating a balanced diet in the Western world. We owe it to ourselves, our families and our Lord to fuel our bodies with sensible food, take regular exercise and look after ourselves. Of course, there is a place for rich treats and celebration food – this book would not exist otherwise – but they can be the exception rather than the rule.

Giving to charities that support developing countries is excellent and there are creative ways of doing this. How about going on a sponsored diet or giving up something for Lent or another period and donating the money saved? Perhaps you could start a group to support each other at your church or in your workplace or neighbourhood.

But let's also get involved in the politics that will make a real impact on the imbalance between rich and poor nations. The *Make Poverty History* campaign offered an unprecedented opportunity for global change to unjust trading practices, national debt and the provision of better aid programmes. It needs to be ongoing.

As we enjoy God's provision for us, let's take the words in Proverbs 29:7 to heart: The righteous care about justice for the poor, but the wicked have no such concern.

Lord of our bodies, help us to re-dedicate them as temples in which to worship you.
Lord of our minds, enable us to find creative ways to meet the needs of those who suffer hardship.
Lord of our spirits, fire our compassion and help us to see the world through your eyes. Amen

In-a-Flap-Jacks

This speedy variation on the traditional flapjack recipe uses the microwave, and can be made when unexpected visitors phone to say they are on their way and you are in a flap!

> If, after your friends have gone home, there are any flapjacks left uneaten, they freeze very well. Simply put in a plastic bag, seal and freeze for up to one month. Thaw for one hour before serving.

Ingredients

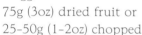

110g (4oz) margarine
110g (4oz) demerara sugar
4 tablespoons golden syrup
225g (8oz) porridge oats
2 teaspoons baking powder
2 teaspoons ground ginger (optional)
1 egg
75g (3oz) dried fruit or
25-50g (1-2oz) chopped
    preserved ginger
    (optional)

Method

1 Line two shallow microwave dishes with clingfilm (I use the lids of two Pyrex casserole dishes. Check that your clingfilm is microwave safe and, if not, thoroughly grease the dishes instead.)
2 In a large bowl melt the margarine, sugar and golden syrup on a HIGH setting (approximately 1 minute depending on the power of the microwave).
3 Stir in the dry ingredients, egg and fruit, or ginger, if using. Mix thoroughly.
4 Divide mixture between two dishes leaving enough room for the mixture to expand. Microwave each for 2-4 minutes depending on the strength of your microwave. When ready, it should begin to firm up, but should not be scorched.
5 Mark each dish into six, before the mixture cools and hardens.
Makes 12.

> Are you tired? Worn out? Burned out on religion? Come to me. Get away with me and you'll recover your life. I'll show you how to take a real rest. Walk with me and work with me – watch how I do it. Learn the unforced rhythms of grace. I won't lay anything heavy or ill-fitting on you. Keep company with me and you'll learn to live freely and lightly.
>
> Matthew 11:28-30 (The Message)

Crisis... all the Choir had arrived at the little church an hour's drive from home where we were presenting the Christian musical, *From Pharaoh to Freedom* by Roger Jones. We had rearranged the furniture, set up our own PA system, laid out all the props... Where was my conductor's copy marked with all the alterations, repeats and special cues?

I insisted I had brought it – someone must have it. *Show me your books, search your seats, the floor, your bags!* Panic.

Near to tears, I scribbled the basic 'Stand, Sit' commands onto a spare copy with minutes to go. Then someone prayed with me and I stood up and conducted an almost flawless (for us!) performance relying on my memory and the Lord. And where was the missing book? On my desk at home under a pile of papers.

I knew exactly how it had happened. After some last minute rubbing out (Slower Colin! Girls – dance! Party poppers at end?) I remembered the Narrator wanted extra words to introduce the characters, so I took the book (already ticked off on my lengthy checklist...) to the study.

While at my tired old computer I also produced posters for Mum's Coffee Morning and tried to transfer large files of photos for my craft business from one program to another. Oh yes, and phoned some elderly friends who had recently had a health scare.

An unwanted caller distracted me and then it was time to get a meal before we set off. Too many balls to juggle...

That morning I had prayed that the Lord would show me clearly what to do with a brilliant idea (or so I thought) for the next special choir event. It would involve a great deal of hard work, not only for me but for others who were already over-stretched. And the others had reservations...

Now I had my answer.

Why do we run ourselves into the ground trying to do too much? For me it is difficult to let go of 'good' ideas – and to say 'No!' God doesn't expect us to be all things to all people all the time. Really he doesn't!

Help us, Lord, to listen to what you want us to do and to get our priorities right. Just that. Amen

Lemon Delight Pudding

When I was on my final teaching practice, staying miles away from
college and friends, my landlady fed me this pudding once a week,
much to my delight. The sponge and lemon sauce separate out during cooking.

 Serve with single cream or crème fraîche
for a delicious treat.

Ingredients
150g (5oz) caster sugar
50g (2oz) margarine or butter
Juice and zest of one large lemon
50g (2oz) self-raising flour, sieved
2 medium eggs, separated
200ml (⅓ pint) milk

Method
1 Preheat oven to gas mark 2/150°C/300°F.
2 Cream sugar and margarine until light and fluffy.
3 Stir in lemon juice and zest, then add flour and egg yolks
  and mix well.
4 Stir in milk.
5 Beat egg whites in a separate bowl until stiff, then fold
  carefully into mixture using a metal spoon. Do not worry
  about the curdled appearance.
6 Pour the mixture into a well-greased ovenproof dish. Place
  the dish in a deep roasting tin and put it in the oven.
  Carefully pour boiling water into the tin to come
  halfway up the dish (creating a bain marie).
  Bake for 30-40 minutes until golden brown.
  Serves 3-4.

When did you last delight in something? What was it?

~ a new-born baby?
~ a lovely meal prepared by someone else?
~ a chance meeting with an old friend?
~ a co-ordinated outfit for a special occasion?

A character in a television play (*Winter Solstice* by Rosamund Pilcher) said to a young woman, 'The gift I gave you at your Christening was endless fun. What happened to it?'

When did you last have fun... let your hair down... enjoy a belly laugh? I giggled helplessly with my two granddaughters recently over a word game that had spiralled downwards into absurdity. And not only did I feel physically better for it but it also bonded us closer together. The eight-year-old apparently went on to quote me to all her friends and acquaintances which could be a bit embarrassing next time I see them...

Jesus had a great sense of humour – just look at some of the exaggerated illustrations in his stories, such as the plank in someone's eye or the camel trying to squeeze through the eye of a needle.

'Delight' is defined as 'a cause or source of great pleasure'. A verse from Deuteronomy (30:9-10) reminds us 'The Lord will again delight in you and make you prosperous... if you... turn to the Lord your God with all your heart and with all your soul'. Isn't it incredible to think that God actually delights in us.

Why not grab a Concordance and look up all the passages which mention *delight* or *joy* and reflect for a while on how to share your delight in God with some of the downcast people in your area?

Alternatively, put on a CD or find a song book and lift your own heart in praise to our maker.

You, Lord, are the greatest King above all others and you hold the depths of the earth in your hand. Praise you, Father God, for the delightful things you have created for our pleasure. We just want to sing with joy, Lord, when we realise how much you delight in us. Amen!

Make a Date Loaf

This is a good cake to have on standby as it improves in the tin after a few days and becomes sticky and more-ish. It will also freeze well. I have sometimes quadrupled the recipe to sell on cake stalls.

Add chopped walnuts to the mixture for a nutty taste.

Ingredients
175g (6oz) ready-pitted dates
150ml (¼ pint) water
110g (4oz) granulated sugar
175g (6oz) plain flour
25g (1oz) margarine
1 teaspoon baking powder
½ teaspoon bicarbonate of soda
1 large egg, beaten

Method
1 Preheat oven to gas mark 2/150°C/300°F. Grease and line a medium-sized loaf tin.
2 Roughly chop dates and place in pan with water and sugar. Bring to the boil and simmer for a few minutes.
3 Sift the flour into a bowl. Rub in the margarine, baking powder and bicarbonate of soda.
4 Add beaten egg and date mixture, and stir until all ingredients are well combined.
5 Turn into tin and bake for 1–1¼ hours until the top springs back.
6 Allow to cool in the tin for a few minutes, then finish cooling on a wire rack.
7 Serve sliced and buttered.
Makes 10-12 slices.

> Daniel… went home to his upstairs room where the windows opened towards Jerusalem. Three times a day he got down on his knees and prayed, giving thanks to his God, just as he had done before.
>
> Daniel 6:10 (NIV)

There was a business man who used to write FSHG in his appointment diary. This always puzzled his secretary, but his schedule was so hectic that he knew that if he didn't make an appointment for the Father, Son and Holy Ghost, his time with God would get completely crowded out.

Do you have a regular date with God? Is there a time each day when you meet with him?

Daniel was in a sticky situation. He was such a popular, sensible young man that King Darius was planning to give him a top job in government. And that made others so jealous that they wanted to destroy him.

Instead of panicking, and despite the threat of being thrown to the lions for praying to God and not to the king, he set himself to pray three times each day, and he was not afraid to pray where he would be seen by others.

Daniel was at a crisis point but, because of his devotion to God, prayer remained a routine part of his life. And, as you know, God honoured his prayers and closed the mouths of the lions.

It is in our regular quiet times with God that we will hear his voice most clearly and build up a picture of where he wants us to be and what he is planning for our lives.

So whatever else threatens to crowd your day, make that date with God top priority and the rest will flow that bit more easily. And if you are too busy to talk to God, then perhaps you are TOO busy!

Faithful God, forgive me for the times I neglect you, when I allow worldly things to sweep me away. Thank you that you are always there waiting for me to keep my date with you. Amen

Merry Muffins

These make a welcome change from mince pies when friends and relations drop by at Christmas time. They freeze well – simply pop in the microwave for a few seconds to serve warm with coffee. Also great for breakfast.

Serve with freshly brewed coffee for a seasonal elevenses between wrapping presents.

Ingredients

1 eating apple
225g (8oz) self-raising flour
½ teaspoon baking powder
3 teaspoons mixed spice
50g (2oz) soft brown sugar
2 large eggs, beaten
75g (3oz) butter or margarine, melted and cooled
200ml (7fl oz) Greek yogurt
110g (4oz) raisins
110g (4oz) dried ready-to-eat cranberries
4 tablespoons mincemeat
1 tablespoon brandy, sherry or spiced cordial

Method

1 Preheat oven to gas mark 5/190°C/375°F. Place ten large paper muffin cases in muffin tin.
2 Core and chop apple finely, leaving skin on.
3 Sift flour, baking powder and spice into bowl and make a well in the middle.
4 Place sugar, eggs, butter or margarine, yogurt, fruits, mincemeat and brandy in well and stir until just combined. Do not over mix.
5 Divide between the paper muffin cases and bake for 25 minutes until well-risen and golden.
6 Cool on wire rack.

Makes 10 muffins.

A cheerful heart brings a smile to your face… a cheerful heart fills the day with song.

Proverbs 15:13a and 15b (The Message)

There used to be a Palm Tree poster that said: 'If you see someone without a smile give them one of yours!'

A character in a book that I read recently was smiling at everyone on the London Underground simply because she felt happy. This was not well received however and one woman growled at her, 'How can you grin when John Lennon has just been shot?'

Of course, it isn't appropriate to go round with a permanent grin on our face when other people might be in despair. As someone who has occasionally suffered with clinical depression, I am not in a position to be glib. But, as a verse from Nehemiah reminds us, 'The joy of the Lord is your strength' (Nehemiah 8:10).

And when we know the Lord our underlying sense of peace and purpose should mean that joy is just waiting to bubble up and find expression.

Lots of people go to church at Christmas because they enjoy the uplifting music. Perhaps they are reassured by the words of carols like 'God rest you merry, gentlemen, let nothing you dismay'. The hope and joy we have in the Lord is more certain and more lasting than that quoted by the secular songs. 'Have yourself a merry little Christmas' always sounds a bit hollow to me.

Perhaps this Christmas we could all look closer at the words of the carols we sing and let our hearts soar upwards at the glorious truth that the birth of one special baby means hope for everyone.

Joy to the world, the Lord has come
Let earth receive her king
Let every heart prepare him room
And heaven and nature sing
And heaven and nature sing
And heaven, and heaven and nature sing!

(Isaac Watts 1674-1748)

Mini Melting Moments

In my folder of puddings and cakes collected over the years, is a precious booklet made by my daughter when she was at primary school. Its title is *Resipies for Yong Cookers*, and these are her little biscuits that disappear as fast as they are made.

For a thoughtful small gift, place a few 'melting moments' in the centre of a good-sized square of cellophane, draw the corners up, and tie off with a bow of pretty ribbon.

Try rolled oats, toasted medium oatmeal or crushed crispy cereal instead of coconut. If you use cereal, eat the 'melting moments' on the same day so the cereal stays crisp.

Ingredients
225g (8oz) butter
175g (6oz) caster sugar
1 egg
½ teaspoon vanilla essence
225g (8oz) self-raising flour
25g (1oz) desiccated coconut

Method
1 Preheat oven to gas mark 5/190°C/375°F. Grease two baking trays.
2 Cream butter and sugar together until light and fluffy. Beat in egg and vanilla essence.
3 Stir in flour to make a smooth dough, and divide into about 40 balls. Roll each ball in coconut.
4 Place balls on baking trays, spaced apart, and bake for 10 minutes until golden. Cool for a couple of minutes, then transfer to wire rack to finish cooling.
Makes 40.

'There is a time for everything, and a season for every activity under the heaven: ...
a time to weep and a time to laugh, a time to mourn and a time to dance...'

Ecclesiastes 3:1-4 (NIV)

My friend Cynthia liked to remember 'frozen moments' – those times when something special happens that touches us and lifts our spirits. I prefer to call them 'melting moments' and sometimes they catch us unawares even in the midst of difficulties or even tragedy. Some of my favourite melting moments are:

A walk in beautiful countryside on a frosty New Year's Day with friends I don't see very often.

The hug of a friend who couldn't find words to say when someone we both loved died after a long painful illness.

The whole family chasing my Nan's hat along a seafront in a high wind...

What are your melting moments? Why not jot some of them down and then pause for a moment to thank God for the gift of happy memories.

Thank You, Father, for the precious things of life and thank You for friends and family to share our melting moments. Remind us, Lord, to value our relationships and to build each other up through the good times and the bad. For the sake of Jesus who walks beside us every moment of every day. Amen

Mixed Berry Mess

This is an interesting cross between traditional Eton Mess and Scottish cranachan. The finished dish should not look a mess, as the term only means a portion of semi-solid or pulpy food.

 To make your own meringues, whisk 2 egg whites in a clean bowl to form stiff peaks. Gradually stir in 110g (4oz) caster sugar and continue to whisk until stiff again. Put dessertspoonfuls of the mixture onto a baking tray lined with foil, and cook at gas mark 2/150°C/300°F for 30 minutes.

Ingredients
350g (12oz) frozen or fresh mixed summer fruits
1-2 tablespoons port or red fruit cordial
75g (3oz) medium oatmeal
284ml (10fl oz) double cream
6 small meringues or 3 meringue baskets,
   broken into pieces
Lemon balm or mint leaves
   to decorate (optional)

Method
1 Defrost the summer fruits, if frozen, and drain. Reserve a few for decoration.
2 Pour port or cordial over the fruit, cover and chill.
3 Toast oatmeal under grill and allow to cool.
4 Whisk cream until it just holds its shape, then gently fold in marinated fruit, oatmeal and meringues.
5 Spoon into individual dishes and serve immediately, decorated with lemon balm or mint leaves if available.
Serves 4-5.

> **Everything should be done in a fitting and orderly way.**
> I Corinthians 14:40 (NIV)

> **For God is not a God of disorder but of peace.**
> I Corinthians 14:33 (NIV)

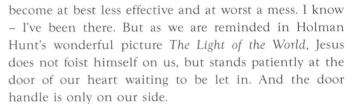

I've turned out my study-cum-workroom at last, and oh the relief of order restored! Now my silk painting work is at one end and my writing and teaching at the other. Now I'll be able to put my hand on the equipment or documents I need straight away without wasting frustrating minutes (hours... days...) searching for them.

My favourite fridge magnet says, 'Dull women have immaculate houses' but I know I use it as an excuse for letting housework go in favour of indulging my creativity.

So – when I finally sat down with a coffee in my spick-and-span workplace I looked again at the story of how God created order out of chaos to see if I could learn something new. And guess what! The first thing the Lord did was to put the light on!

How often we muddle along not only in physical mess but also in mental and spiritual confusion because we don't allow the light of Christ into our lives. The trouble with my workroom was that when I turned the light on it simply showed up the disorder and the dust so I preferred to make hasty dashes in and out and postpone getting down to proper work.

When we neglect spiritual things and wander away from regular fellowship with the Lord and other Christians our lives are likely to become at best less effective and at worst a mess. I know – I've been there. But as we are reminded in Holman Hunt's wonderful picture *The Light of the World*, Jesus does not foist himself on us, but stands patiently at the door of our heart waiting to be let in. And the door handle is only on our side.

Another magnet says, 'My kitchen was tidy last week – sorry you missed it!' Jesus cares much more about us as individuals than about the state of our houses and if our lives are in a mess – he wants to help us clean them up.

From now on, I'm going to try to be more consistent in keeping both my home and my life in a tidier state.

Lord, because we are human we know we will fail at times; thank you so much that you forgive us over and over again. Help us to learn from our mistakes and to depend more and more on you for strength to achieve all you want us to do. Amen

Raspberry Butterflies

My young friend Charlotte thought these cakes
were the very best of an assortment of goodies
I baked for a picnic.

 These pretty cakes appeal to children and
would look good on your Easter tea table.

Ingredients

110g (4oz) soft margarine
110g (4oz) caster sugar
2 medium eggs
1 teaspoon vanilla essence
110g (4oz) self-raising flour
½ teaspoon baking powder

For the filling:
50g (2oz) butter, softened
½ teaspoon vanilla essence
110g (4oz) icing sugar
Fresh raspberries and chocolate
  matchsticks to decorate

Method

1 Preheat oven to gas mark 5/190°C/375°F. Line a 12-hole
  bun tin with paper cake-cases.
2 Place margarine, sugar, eggs and vanilla essence in a bowl.
  Sift in flour and baking powder, and beat together
  until blended.
3 Divide mixture between the 12 paper cases and bake in
  centre of oven for 20 minutes until well risen and golden.
4 Cool on wire rack.
5 For the filling, beat butter and vanilla essence together and
  gradually sift in icing sugar.
6 Cut tops from cooled cakes and slice each top in half to
  make wings.
7 Place a blob of icing on each cake, replace wings and
  arrange three smallish raspberries down the centre to make
  the body of the butterfly. Add chocolate matchsticks to
  look like antennae.
  Makes 12.

Death has been swallowed up in victory.

1 Corinthians 15:54b (NIV)

My brother's wife, Su-Ann, was diagnosed with cancer in her early thirties when their daughter, Gemma, was only three. Many, many prayers were said and one day as I battled with the Lord for her I was given a striking mental picture of Su sitting by a stream, dressed all in white, under beautiful green trees and in dappled sunlight. Though this was some years ago that picture is as vivid now as then.

She had recently become a Christian and been baptised. A sense of peace flooded over me as I recognised that whatever happened she would find healing – either on earth or more completely in heaven.

At Su's funeral a few months later we were able to rejoice as we sang, 'When the roll is called up yonder I'll be there...' even while we grieved for her loss.

The transformation of her poor diseased body into the bright, light perfection of her resurrection body reminded me of the changes a butterfly goes through. That insignificant little green caterpillar confined to its leaves will become the beautiful free-flying creature that we all admire.

Since starting to paint on silk I have become fascinated by the *bombyx mori* moth which changes from a fat,

hairless and deeply unattractive grub into a cocoon which will yield many metres of the finest silk! The life cycle of butterflies and moths seems to me to be a parable of the way we can be transformed. The little caterpillar confined to munching its way through umpteen leaves will seem dead to the world in its chrysalis stage but then one day will burst forth to be the beautiful creature we enjoy watching so much around our flower gardens.

At Easter time, it is good to remember that because of Jesus' death and resurrection, if we trust him as our Lord and Saviour we too will be freed from the limitations of our physical bodies. And one day we will be perfect creatures who will delight our maker as we praise him with all the other believers.

Lord, I'm looking forward to being a beautiful butterfly in your kingdom. Thank you, loving Father, that you are changing me by the power of your Spirit. Amen

Rest and Be Thankful Chocolate Cake

When you need to have a break and take
stock of where you are in the day's tasks,
enjoy a slice with a cup of tea.

To make chocolate fudge icing, put 110g
(4oz) granulated sugar and 115ml (4fl oz)
milk into a pan. Simmer for 9 minutes,
then add 150g (5oz) plain chocolate,
50g (2oz) butter and 2 tablespoons
double cream. Leave to cool and then
spread over the cake.

Ingredients
150g (5oz) self-raising flour
75g (3oz) drinking chocolate
175g (6oz) caster sugar
175g (6oz) butter or margarine at room temperature
3 large eggs
3 tablespoons boiling water

Method
1 Preheat oven to gas mark 4/180°C/350°F. Grease and line a
  20cm (8in) round cake tin.
2 Sift flour and drinking chocolate into a large mixing bowl.
3 Add all other ingredients and blend together. Beat for a
  couple of minutes until smooth.
4 Turn into tin and bake for about
  45-60 minutes until a fine skewer inserted in the middle
  comes out clean.
5 Leave in tin for a few minutes, then cool on wire rack.
6 Ice with your favourite icing or melted chocolate.
  This quick and easy cake keeps well in a tin.

> But they that wait upon the Lord shall renew their strength, they shall mount up with wings as eagles; they shall run and not be weary, and they shall walk and not faint.
>
> Isaiah 40:31 (AV)

In several conspicuous places, I have written a phrase from a Marilyn Baker song...
'Rest in His love, relax in His care.'

How often I need that reminder as I flit from one task to another whilst fretting about a third. Lately, I have become aware that I waste more time and energy worrying about how to achieve all my goals than in actually getting on with the steps that make them attainable.

In Argyllshire, in the wonderful Highlands of Scotland, there is a viewpoint called 'Rest and Be Thankful'. It's on a high road originally used by cattle drovers taking their stock to market. No doubt the men and animals alike were glad of the rest when they had slogged up the steep hill and would be thankful that the remainder of their journey was downhill.

Jesus often withdrew from the pressures of his ministry especially to pray to his Father. The trouble was even he couldn't always achieve the quality time he needed. Once, when he had encouraged his disciples to take some time out with him, they were followed and Jesus ended up performing the miracle of feeding thousands of physically and spiritually hungry people! (Mark 6:30-44)

Taking time out every so often to evaluate our lives before the Lord is very healthy. We may need a few days' retreat or simply a long walk by ourselves. Or perhaps we will only have the opportunity to follow the example of Susannah Wesley whose children – including the famous John and Charles – knew that when she threw her apron over her head she was not to be disturbed as she communed with the Lord!

Thank You, Lord, for opportunities to work, rest and play; help us to get the balance right and to be sure that the busyness we get caught up in is what you want us to be doing. May we find opportunities to be alone with you and to listen to your voice. Amen

Scones of Splendour

These are rather richer than the traditional recipe and make a good teatime treat with a home-made preserve. I like Morello cherry jam, but try your own favourite.

Dip your scone cutter in flour before cutting out the rounds. This will prevent the cutter from sticking to the dough.

Ingredients
225g (8oz) self-raising flour
½ teaspoon salt
50g (2oz) margarine
50g (2oz) caster sugar
75g (3oz) dried ready-to-eat cranberries
1 medium egg
2–3 tablespoons milk to mix

Method
1 Preheat oven to gas mark 7/220°C/425°F. Grease a baking tray.
2 Sift flour and salt into a bowl and rub in the margarine.
3 Stir in sugar and cranberries.
4 Beat egg, then add it with enough milk to make a soft dough.
5 Turn onto floured surface, knead lightly and roll out to about 2cm (¾in) thickness.
6 Cut into 6 rounds with a 6cm (2½in) medium cutter.
7 Brush with a little more egg and milk, if liked.
8 Bake for 10–15 minutes.
9 Cool on a wire rack.

Makes 6 large scones.

Praise the LORD, O my soul. O LORD my God, you are very great;
you are clothed with splendour and majesty.

Psalm 104:1 (NIV)

I like to have breakfast with God. Sitting in a comfortable chair with my cereal, orange juice and tea, I read, pray and meditate and this feels as acceptable as sharing a meal with a friend or having a business meeting in a restaurant.

However, one morning, having finished eating, I noticed that I had snagged a fingernail and, still chatting to the Lord, I reached for an emery board and began buffing away.

Then I put it down again with a jolt. What was I doing? Would I give myself a manicure whilst talking to the Queen? No way. How much less appropriate then whilst in the presence of the King of Kings! I reddened in awe.

Our Sunday School children sing, 'Our God is a great big God... and he holds us in his hands'. That little song seems to put our relationship with a loving Father God into perspective. Not only has he created a whole world to hold in his hands but he cares enough about every last tiny baby as if it was the only one. Now isn't that genuinely splendid?

I remember being much in awe of my father when I was a child. He seemed to know so much and I never doubted any fact that he told me whether it was the name of a wild flower or a piece of family history.

He was also a strict disciplinarian and I knew that if I crossed him I was in for it! Underpinning all that, even if I thought some of his punishments harsh, I never doubted that he loved me. Our heavenly Father, infinitely greater than any earthly one, will never be anything other than totally and utterly reliable.

Lord, you are awesome, magnificent, splendid. I can't find words to describe your majesty. Thank you that I can come into your royal presence just as I am with no pretence. I worship you, Lord, for who you are. Amen

53

Speedy Turnovers

This easy pudding uses bread instead of pastry and the turnovers are, in fact, sandwiches fried in butter reminiscent of eggy or fairy bread. It is a good way of using up stale bread or small quantities of fruit. The turnovers are quite rich and would make a different light lunch for one using a quarter of the ingredients.

> These are delicious served with ice-cream or Greek-style yogurt. I like a wedge of cheese served with an apple turnover, or you could put crumbled Cheshire or Caerphilly with the apple inside the turnover. Other filling ideas include pear and flaked almonds in granary bread or slices of banana and three or four squares of plain chocolate.

Ingredients

8 slices medium-sliced white bread
Butter for spreading and frying
Spices to taste e.g. ginger, cinnamon, nutmeg
Your choice of stewed or tinned fruit,
    or fruit pie-filling
4 medium eggs
4 tablespoons caster sugar
4 tablespoons whole milk or single cream

Method

1 Butter all the slices of bread on one side only, then cut off the crusts.

2 Place four slices of bread on a board, butter side up. Mix a little spice into your chosen fruit filling and divide between the four slices. Use the other four slices of bread, butter side down, as lids. Press together to seal the edges.

3 Beat eggs, sugar and milk or cream together in a shallow dish, then place sandwiches in mixture, turning to ensure they are evenly coated.

4 Melt butter in a large pan and, when starting to sizzle, fry turnovers on a low heat until golden on both sides, turning carefully.
Serves 4.

> Therefore, if anyone is in Christ, he is a new creation; the old has gone, the new has come!
>
> 2 Corinthians 5:17 (NIV)

At a New Year party, we each wrote our resolutions on slips of paper, and on a separate slip wrote how we were planning to achieve them. We then mixed them up and read them out at random. The results were hilarious:

To finish the kitchen off so that the nagging will stop – *by walking to the shops instead of taking the car.*

To chat up as many girls as possible – *by joining the Mums and Toddlers Group.*

To lose a stone – *by having different people round for a meal each month.*

My own resolution was to get on top of the housework. Housework and I don't mix.

Recently I tried a new miracle bathroom cleaner but after the first attempt, I was not impressed. It was quite expensive so some time later I had another go – this time reading the instructions properly and also putting a bit more elbow grease into the job. Now royalty can come and have a shower in my bathroom – or at least my stepson, Simon, who is taller than us and can see the parts I usually overlook!

The instructions on the miracle cleaner were quite clear when I bothered to read them. God's instructions in the Bible are quite clear too, but we need to take time to understand how they apply to us.

God often expects us to do our part in working miracles! He doesn't *need* our involvement or help, but he loves to work with and through his children. When the blind man was healed by Jesus putting mud on his eyes he was told to go and wash it off in the pool of Siloam before he could see (John 9). And when the paralysed man was healed, his friends had first to carry him to Jesus and then lower him through the roof into the crowded house.

We need to be prepared to put spiritual as well as physical effort into our activities and to work with the Lord to achieve our goals.

Lord, help us to listen to the inner voice which prompts us when we need to turn over a new leaf.
May our first resolution always be to serve you as you deserve. Amen

Spiced Easter Biscuits

These useful little biscuits keep well in a tin and
can be eaten at any time of year. They are thought to have originated as an
Easter tradition in the West Country.

 Use dried cranberries in place of the candied peel.

Ingredients

110g (4oz) butter
75g (3oz) golden caster sugar
1 medium egg
200g (7oz) plain flour
1 level teaspoon mixed spice
50g (2oz) chopped candied peel
50g (2oz) currants
1-2 tablespoons milk
Extra sugar for sprinkling

Method

1 Preheat oven to gas mark 6/200°C/400°F. Grease two
baking trays.
2 Cream butter and sugar together until light and fluffy.
3 Separate egg and beat yolk into mixture.
4 Sift flour and spice together and add to mixture with fruit.
5 Stir together with enough milk to make a stiff dough.
6 Knead lightly on floured surface until smooth, then roll
out to about 5mm (¼in) thickness.
7 Cut into 20 rounds using 7.5cm (3in) fluted cutter
and bake for 8 minutes.
8 Lightly beat egg white. Remove biscuits from
oven, then brush with egg white and
sprinkle with sugar.
9 Return to oven for a further
2-3 minutes until golden.
10 Cool on wire rack.
Makes 20 biscuits.

> When the Sabbath was over, Mary Magdalene, Mary the mother of James,
> and Salome bought spices so that they might go to anoint Jesus' body.
>
> Mark 16:1 (NIV)

'Variety is the spice of life', people say. We may pass on a spicy piece of news or talk about spicing things up.

Did you know that nutmeg was once the third most valuable commodity in the world, exceeded only by silver and gold? Spices have always been highly valued, both as preservatives and also to make bland food taste more interesting. They have also been used worldwide for medicinal purposes – ginger and fennel were used as cures for wind, garlic was eaten to thin the blood and cloves were used as an antiseptic.

In the Middle Ages spices were brought to Europe from the East along the famous Silk Road. Christopher Columbus stumbled across America whilst looking for the Spice Islands.

When the women went to the tomb on the third day after Jesus' crucifixion they were simply going to anoint his body according to their tradition.

This, they believed, would be the last loving service they could perform for him. Their devotion was rewarded by being some of the first to make the astounding and joyful discovery – he was risen! The preserving spices weren't needed; his resurrection body would live forever without them.

At Easter time both hot-cross buns and Easter biscuits remind us of the sacrifice Jesus made for us. Maybe we can think of some different ways that we can be like spice in a needy world – preserving standards, healing hurts and giving people a new taste for the things of God.

Precious Saviour, thank you that you died and rose again for us. May we share the Easter message with everyone we meet and spice up their lives with the best news of all. Amen

Strawberry Shortbread Hearts

Don't just keep these for Valentine's Day – children and adults will love a reminder of how much they mean to you, when you serve these special treats.

To make a heart template, fold a 7.5cm (3in) square of paper in half. Draw half a heart shape up to the crease. Keeping the fold, cut round the shape. Draw around the paper heart onto the washed lid of a used plastic ice-cream carton and cut out the shape. You now have a washable template that you can place on the shortbread dough.

Ingredients

For Shortbread:
175g (6oz) plain flour
50g (2oz) ground almonds
50g (2oz) caster sugar
150g (5oz) butter

To finish:
450g (1lb) fresh strawberries
25g (1oz) caster sugar
275ml (½ pint)
   double cream

Method

1 Preheat oven to gas mark 3/170°C/325°F. Lightly grease a baking tray.
2 Sift flour into bowl and add ground almonds and sugar. Rub butter into mixture, then bring together with hands until it forms a soft dough. Knead lightly until smooth.
3 On a lightly floured surface, roll out the shortbread mixture to about 5mm (¼in) thick and cut into eight hearts using a cutter or template.
4 Transfer to the baking tray, spacing them well apart. Bake for 20–30 minutes until golden. Transfer carefully to wire cooling rack.
5 Purée half the prepared strawberries with the sugar. Whip the cream until firm.
6 When the shortbread is cool, place four hearts on individual plates. Spoon on some cream, some purée and a few sliced strawberries, then top with the remaining hearts. Finish off with a whirl of whipped cream and some whole strawberries.
7 Dust with sifted icing sugar, if liked.
Serves 4.

> The Lord said to Moses, 'Tell the Israelites to bring me an offering. You are to receive the offering for me from each man whose heart prompts him to give'.
>
> Exodus 25:1-2 (NIV)

The story is told of a little boy who wanted to make a Valentine's card for each of his classmates. His Mum's heart sank as she knew he had few real friends and was usually left out of playtime activities. Still, night after night she helped him to make 30 individual cards and on Valentine's Day she planned a special tea to make up for the disappointment he was sure to feel when he returned home empty-handed.

The children came out of school and as usual the boy tagged along at the back of the crowd. As he neared his mother she heard him murmuring, 'Not one, not one' and prepared to comfort him.

But, when he reached her his face was glowing with delight. 'Not one, Mum. I didn't forget one!'

Who do you know who has a big heart?

When I was a single parent and my daughter Katherine was still quite young, a Christian I barely knew at the time heard I was looking for work but had no car. Since her husband and father sadly had died within a short time of each other, she offered me her father's Mini completely free. This enabled me to take a well-paid and challenging teaching job 16 miles from home, which would have been impossible without transport. I stayed there for seven years in the certain knowledge that I was in the right place at the right time.

That person had a big heart.

How big is your heart? Big enough to be generous even when it hurts? Big enough to forgive over and over again? Big enough to go the extra mile – and then another? Jesus did all of those things and he also went on to say that whatever we do for the least of his people we do for him.

Lord, your heart was big enough to die for every one of us, our hearts seem puny little things by comparison. Help us to expand our hearts to show love to those who need your touch, knowing that we do it for you. Amen

Sunday Sundaes

When the head cook has been providing meals all week an easy pudding on Sunday can be a boon. Many fast food outlets and family pubs offer exciting make-your-owns but home-made sundaes are only as limited as your own imagination.

 These sundaes are delicious when topped with a home-made sauce, but make it in advance so that you can keep your Sunday restful!

Ingredients

Good quality soft-scoop ice-cream
A selection of:
    chopped jelly; fresh or tinned fruit; grated chocolate, chocolate drops or flakes; chopped nuts or desiccated coconut; small sweets; crunchy cereal
    Bottled sauces:
    chocolate, strawberry or butterscotch, or use one of the home-made sauces described on the right
Squirty aerosol cream

Method

Combine your own favourite ingredients in a tall sundae glass. Add one of the following sauces and then top with cream.

Chocolate sauce:

Melt 50g (2oz) plain chocolate with 4 tablespoons of double cream and 10g (½oz) butter, stirring until smooth.

Caramel sauce:

Heat 4 tablespoons double cream with 3 heaped tablespoons brown sugar and 20g (¾oz) butter. Stir until the sugar dissolves and the sauce is smooth.

Strawberry sauce:

Wash and hull 450g (1lb) fresh strawberries. Purée together with 25g (1oz) sifted icing sugar. Sieve before serving.

Some of the rules for Sunday at home did not make much sense when I was a child. My Nan didn't knit, I couldn't whistle and we certainly never played cards, a favourite pastime any other day. Some of my Sunday School friends couldn't watch television either.

Now perhaps we've gone to the other extreme with shopping centres buzzing, as much traffic on the road as any weekday and families pursuing leisure activities together instead of attending church.

It is so easy to lower our own standards to fit in with the world around us but consider this quote from John Stott (in *Issues Facing Christians Today*).

> '...if society deteriorates and its standards decline till it becomes like a dark night or a stinking fish, there is no sense in blaming society... The question to ask is, 'Where is the Church? Why are the salt and light of Jesus Christ not permeating and changing our society?'

In the 80s and 90s, the Keep Sunday Special Campaign warned that the destruction of Sunday as a day of rest and recreation would have dire consequences for family life in Britain. Is that warning now being lived out?

As well as being more careful in our own use of Sunday perhaps we could think of some creative ways to make it a family-orientated day again.

What about a picnic in the park after morning church to which Sunday School children invite their non-attending parents? Or a monthly roast dinner followed by games in the winter? Just taking the pressure off hard-pushed parents is often enough to let them see Christianity in action.

P.S. On a more frivolous note – I once adopted an unwanted spaniel called Cindy. Not liking the name, I changed it to Sundae as it sounded similar. I often wondered if the neighbours thought I had taken religious fervour to extremes as I stood at the back door on Saturday nights calling, 'Sundae, come on Sundae. Hurry up, Sundae!'

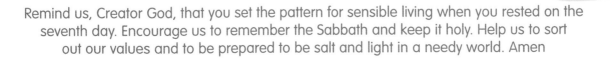

Remind us, Creator God, that you set the pattern for sensible living when you rested on the seventh day. Encourage us to remember the Sabbath and keep it holy. Help us to sort out our values and to be prepared to be salt and light in a needy world. Amen

Sunshine Drizzle Cake

Here's an easy tray-bake to brighten the dullest day.
Why not invite someone round to share it?

 For a sharper taste, substitute lemon
juice for some of the orange.

Ingredients

1 large orange
110g (4oz) margarine
110g (4oz) caster sugar
2 large eggs
225g (8oz) self-raising flour
6 tablespoons milk
225g (8oz) icing sugar

Method

1 Preheat oven to gas mark 4/180°C/350°F. Grease a shallow
  Swiss roll tin, 28cm x 17.5cm (11in x 7in), and line with
  baking parchment, leaving a little sticking out at either end.
2 Grate zest from the orange. Cut in half and squeeze out
  the juice to use later.
3 Cream margarine, sugar and zest together until light
  and fluffy.
4 Beat eggs and then add to mixture with a little flour,
  beating until smooth.
5 Fold in remaining sifted flour and add the milk.
6 Turn into tin and smooth the surface with a palette knife.
7 Bake in centre of oven for 25-30 minutes until golden and
  springy to the touch.
8 Place the tin on a wire cooling rack.
9 Sift the icing sugar into a bowl and add the orange juice,
  avoiding any membrane. Beat until smooth, then spread
  over warm cake.
10 Leave in tin until cool, and the icing is set, then
  carefully lift out and remove paper.

Makes 14-16 slices.

I have fond memories of my Dad gazing out of a seaside guest house window and saying gloomily, 'It's that fine wetting sort of rain'. We used to tease him. Wasn't all rain 'wetting'? But we knew what he meant. A real downpour either caused you to stay in and do a jigsaw or to brave it and dash to the nearest cinema. Better still, you waited for another of his idiosyncratic weather phenomena 'the clearing-up shower' and then made for the beach before the clouds could change their mind.

But drizzle, that spirit-lowering, neither-one-thing-nor-the-other kind of rain, meant endless hours trooping damply round shops or steaming up the car getting irritable with each other.

And yet, as St Paul reminds us, we can learn to be thankful in all things and turn the rain to sunshine.

The wettest holiday my daughter, Katherine, and I ever spent was with my brother's family. It poured for six-and-a-half days out of the week we stayed in a remote cottage in Scotland. But, oh boy, did we enjoy the half day when the sun shone and the children romped on the golden sands at St Andrews! Not only that but we also found more and more creative ways to pass the rainy times, laughing and playing and growing closer together.

And the children learned the rhyme that my Dad had taught us and which can be applied to more than just the climate...

Whether the weather be cold, whether the weather be hot, we'll weather the weather, whatever the weather, whether we like it or not!

Glad that I live am I, that the sky is blue
Glad for the country lanes and the fall of dew
After the sun the rain, after the rain the sun
This is the way of life till the work be done.

All that we need to do, be we low or high,
Is to see that we grow nearer the sky.

Lizette Woodworth Reese (© 1925 OUP)

Tea and Sympathy Cake

In the days when women stayed at home and baked, Cut-and-Come-Again cakes were kept in a tin for visitors as well as family. It's not a bad tradition to revive. Alternatively, why not take a cake as an icebreaker when you visit someone who needs a sympathetic ear?

Substitute chopped glacé cherries, dates or nuts for some of the mixed dried fruit.

Ingredients

350g (12oz) mixed dried fruit
110g (4oz) light soft brown sugar
110g (4oz) margarine or butter
150ml (¼ pint/5fl oz) water
1 large egg, beaten
225g (8oz) self-raising flour

Method

1 Preheat oven to gas mark 2/150°C/300°F. Grease a 15cm (6in) round cake tin.
2 Put fruit, sugar, margarine and water in saucepan. Bring to the boil and simmer gently for about 20 minutes to plump up the fruit.
3 Allow to cool a little, then add the egg, mix well and stir in the flour.
4 Turn into greased tin, smooth over the top and bake for about 1½ hours until a skewer inserted in the middle of the cake comes out clean.
5 Cool on wire rack.

Makes 8-10 slices.

Carry each other's burdens, and in this way you will fulfil the law of Christ.

Galations 6:2 (NIV)

My husband turned the television on to a football match and then left the room. Returning a few minutes later, he asked me how the game was going. I had no idea.

'But you were watching it!' he exclaimed.

Well no, actually. I might have been gazing at the screen but nothing had gone in – not the score displayed at the top, nor the commentary, nor even which teams were playing (some red ones and some blue ones...?).

Is our concentration sometimes equally lacking when we meet friends? Our minds are elsewhere when we appear to be listening. We've all experienced the person who gives us great eye contact and nods and makes sympathetic noises as we tell our tale, but who spots someone else over our shoulder and soon makes an excuse to be off. Maybe we do this ourselves.

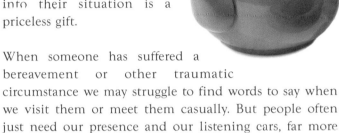

And yet to be able truly to give our full attention to another person and enter into their situation is a priceless gift.

When someone has suffered a bereavement or other traumatic circumstance we may struggle to find words to say when we visit them or meet them casually. But people often just need our presence and our listening ears, far more than our talking mouths.

As some teachers say, 'God gave you two ears, but only one mouth, because he expects you to do twice as much listening as talking!'

Lord, in your earthly life you always made time for people. Help us to develop listening ears and hearts and enable us to be more willing to listen than to speak, for the sake of Jesus who understood suffering and cares about those who suffer today. Amen

The Best Ever No-bake Chocolate Slice!

I have several variations on no-bake cakes that use up broken biscuits, but this is an exceptionally delicious one which I have often made to take away on group holidays, or to sell at coffee mornings.

Ingredients

Base:

110g (4oz) butter or margarine

110g (4oz) granulated sugar

3 rounded dessertspoons cocoa powder

1 medium egg

1 teaspoon vanilla essence

225g (8oz) crushed biscuits, such as Digestive or Nice

75g (3oz) chopped nuts (almonds, hazels, Brazils, walnuts or a combination)

1 tablespoon sherry or brandy (optional)

Topping:

50g (2oz) butter

1 teaspoon finely grated lemon zest

350g (12oz) icing sugar

2 dessertspoons traditional custard powder

4 dessertspoons warm water

175g (6oz) plain chocolate

Method

1 Place butter, sugar and cocoa powder in a medium saucepan and stir over low heat until well blended. Stir in egg and vanilla essence. Continue to cook, stirring for 1 minute, while the mixture thickens.

2 Remove from heat, stir in biscuit crumbs, nuts and alcohol, if using. Mix thoroughly.

3 Turn into a Swiss roll tin 28cm x 17.5cm (11in x 7in), lined with baking parchment or greaseproof paper, and chill until set.

4 For the topping, cream butter with lemon zest until light and fluffy. Sift in the icing sugar and custard powder alternately with the warm water, and beat well.

5 Spread over the base and chill.

6 Melt the chocolate and quickly spread over the topping.

7 Chill again before cutting into squares. Best stored in fridge.

Makes 24 squares.

When I was a child, a shop-bought cake was a treat though we had home-made ones regularly. Now it's the other way round and the cake-stalls at farmers' markets and craft fairs tend to sell out the quickest. To put time and effort into making something special is appreciated by those on the receiving end whether they have bought or been given the goods.

The offering of first-fruits was an acknowledgement by the Israelites that the whole of the harvest was created by and belonged to the Lord. Our own Harvest Festival traditions are dying out as 21st century life relies less and less on conventional farming methods and what were once seasonal fruit and vegetables are now available all year round.

God deserves the very best we can give him and this often means time and effort as well as money and material things, important though they are. Whether we are serving the coffee or preaching a sermon, teaching in Sunday School or mopping the floors, if we put our best into the task then we will honour the Lord.

As my friend, Helen, and I were preparing to lead worship at a special event, we began to doubt that we could match the others that had gone before us. But then Helen reminded me that we can only be ourselves and bring to the Lord our best without worrying about being perfect or comparing ourselves to others.

And I was reminded of Brother Lawrence – the 17th century French monk who wrote a little book called *The Practice of the Presence of God.* Described by others who knew him as a gentle man of joyful spirit, he worked in the monastery kitchen serving over a hundred fellow monks for many years.

He believed that we could not only serve God in the humblest situations, such as peeling the vegetables or scrubbing floors, but also know his peace and presence wherever we find ourselves.

So let's take a leaf out of Brother Lawrence's book and bring our first-fruits to God and our very best effort to everything we do for him.

Lord, sometimes I give you my best, sometimes only my second best and sometimes nothing worth having at all. Help me always to aspire to give my very best for you in all circumstances. Amen.

Tumble-down Cake

The crumbly topping adds interest to this cake, which could also be warmed in the microwave and served as a pudding with custard or clotted cream. It will keep in the fridge for three to four days wrapped in foil, or could be sliced and frozen.

Ingredients

Cake:
175g (6oz) butter at room temperature
175g (6oz) caster sugar
1 teaspoon finely grated lemon zest
3 medium eggs
225g (8oz) self-raising flour

Crumble Topping:
2 large eating apples
75g (3oz) butter or margarine
110g (4oz) plain wholemeal flour
1 teaspoon ground cinnamon
50g (2oz) demerara sugar

Method

1 Preheat oven to gas mark 4/180°C/350°F. Grease and line a loose-bottomed 20cm (8in) round cake tin.
2 Cream butter, sugar and zest together until light and fluffy.
3 Beat eggs together, then gradually add to the mixture with a small amount of flour, to avoid curdling.
4 Fold in remaining flour and spoon into tin, levelling top with the back of a spoon.
5 Peel, core and finely slice the apples and arrange on top of cake mixture.
6 Rub butter, or margarine, roughly into wholemeal flour and cinnamon to give chunky crumble mix. Add demerara sugar and sprinkle over apples.
7 Bake for 1¼ hours until golden. Cool in tin for a few minutes, then leave on a wire rack until cold.

Makes 8-10 slices.

> So if the Son sets you free, you will be free indeed.
> John 8:36 (NIV)

Our holiday flat overlooked the sea, and on a stretch of grass in between a young boy was playing with a remote-controlled helicopter. Time after time, he launched the craft into the wind and ran behind it. Time after time, it veered round then fell to the ground. As I watched him I thought that – like God – the boy seemed to have infinite patience.

Sometimes the Lord sets us off on a promising course, but we think we know best, go our own way and find our plans come to nothing. Then God gives us another chance...

Of course, the boy's skill at the controls could be questioned – unlike God's.

But the other factor, a skittish breeze, can be compared to the influences in life that blow us around if we let them. Unlike the helicopter, we have free will and can choose to go God's way or the way of the world. Eventually the boy gave up, climbed into the family car and was driven away. This won't happen with God! Only when we have handed back control and are flying in his strength, allowing him to steer us, will we know true peace and that sense of soaring above the problems of daily life.

The story is told of a man who fell over a cliff.

He managed to grab hold of a small branch and cried out 'Is there anybody there who can help me?'

'Yes,' came God's voice from above. 'Just let go of the branch and I will save you.'

After a pause, the man called out again 'Is there anybody else up there?'

Don't let's be like that man!

Lord, we know that sometimes we are likely to tumble down in our walk of faith; thank you that you catch us when we fall and set us back up on our feet. Help us to lean on you and allow your guidance and strength to lead us through the pitfalls of life. Amen.

Welcome Rock Cakes

For cakes with a more golden-brown 'finish', dust with demerara sugar instead of granulated.

We used to rustle up these quick, never-fail cakes to welcome people after their journey to the Christian hotel where I once worked. And, unlike their name, they melted in the mouth! How about a plate of them to welcome friends and neighbours when they call in?

Ingredients

225g (8oz) self-raising flour
110g (4oz) margarine
110g (4oz) granulated sugar, plus extra for dusting
175g (6oz) mixed dried fruit
1 egg
Milk to mix

Method

1 Preheat oven to gas mark 7/220°C/425°F. Grease two baking trays.
2 Sift flour into mixing bowl and rub in the margarine.
3 Add sugar and fruit. Make a well in the centre.
4 Beat the egg, then add to the dry ingredients with a little milk to make a stiff consistency.
5 Place the mixture in rough heaps on both baking trays and dust with granulated sugar.
6 Bake for 10 minutes until golden brown.
7 Cool on wire rack.

Makes 18 cakes.

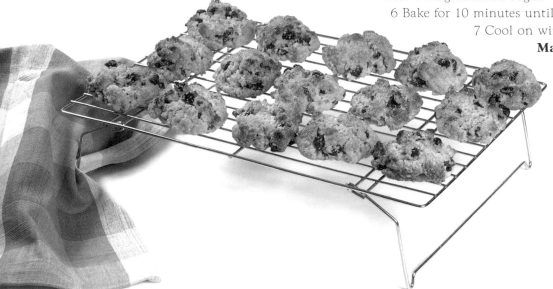

He is the Rock, his works are perfect, and all his ways are just.
A faithful God who does no wrong, upright and just is he.
Deuteronomy 32:4 (NIV)

Dora and Frank (not their real names) were amusingly like a seaside postcard parody. She was large, jolly and loud. He was slight, meek and mild and always seemed to be following in her wake. Then, one day, in an unusual display of emotion, Dora said 'Frank is my Rock. I can trust him completely, he is always there for me' and we viewed them differently from then on.

Maybe you have a human rock in your life? And maybe you are a rock for someone else? Perhaps friends, neighbours or relatives will come to depend on you for practical or emotional help as the years go by and you will be able to show them what your faith means to you.

What a lovely picture the Bible paints of the Lord as an immovable rock, always there, always the same, always dependable.

Hannah, after the birth of her much-longed-for son Samuel, prayed a prayer of praise and thanksgiving. 'There is no-one holy like the LORD'; she sang. 'There is no-one besides you; there is no Rock like our God.'

(I Samuel 2:2, NIV). She hadn't had an easy life and though her dream had now been realised it came with conditions. She would have to let her precious son be parted from her to serve in the temple as she had promised God.

Hannah knew that human relationships, great though they are, will change or waver sometimes. People die, move on, let us down. But her Lord and ours can never do that. Our grandchildren sing, 'Don't build your house on the sandy land' reminding us that we need to build our lives on a solid foundation so that when the storms come – as they will – we will know God's peace deep in our hearts and be anchored firmly to the rock of his love.

I want to sing praises to you, Lord, because you are the Rock of my salvation.
I want to be a rock for others too, Lord, in your strength.
Help me to build my life on your strong foundation so that the storms of life will never shake my faith. Amen.

Useful addresses

The profits from the sale of this book go to support the work of
The Leprosy Mission in hospitals and rehabilitation workshops abroad.

TLM TRADING LIMITED
*To buy books, gifts and craft items made by
leprosy affected people contact us at...*
PO Box 212, Peterborough, PE2 5GD, UK
Tel: 0845 1662253   Fax: 01733 239258
Email: enquiries@tlmtrading.com
www.tlmtrading.com

TLM INTERNATIONAL
80 Windmill Road, Brentford,
Middlesex, TW8 0QH, UK.
Tel: 020 8326 6767   Fax: 020 8326 6777
Email: friends@tlmint.org
www.leprosymission.org

TLM ENGLAND AND WALES
www.leprosymission.org.uk

TLM NORTHERN IRELAND
www.tlm-ni.org

TLM SCOTLAND
www.tlmscotland.org.uk

*The Leprosy Mission has offices all around the world.
Please contact TLM International if you would like contact details
for any of the following offices:*

Africa Regional Office, Australia, Belgium, Canada, Denmark, Finland,
France, Germany, Hungary, India Regional Office, Ireland, Italy,
Netherlands, New Zealand, Portugal, South-East Asia Regional Office,
South Africa, Spain, Sweden, Switzerland, USA (Assoc Org), Zimbabwe